HOW TO OPEN A SUCCESSFUL
CREAMERY

A Comprehensive Guide to Starting, Running and Growing
Your Own Creamery Business

ROGER LOONEY

TABLE OF CONTENTS

INTRODUCTION

The allure of creamy, decadent dairy products has captured the hearts and palates of food enthusiasts for centuries. From rich, velvety cheeses to luxurious, indulgent ice creams, the possibilities for crafting delicious dairy delights are endless. In recent years, there has been a resurgence of interest in artisanal and locally sourced foods, creating a ripe opportunity for aspiring creamery owners to enter the market and share their passion for quality dairy products with the world.

However, starting and operating a creamery is no small feat. It requires careful planning, attention to detail, and a deep understanding of both the art and science of dairy production. That's where Creamery Craft comes in. Whether you're a seasoned dairy professional looking to strike out on your own or a newcomer to the world of creameries, this book serves as your comprehensive roadmap, guiding you through every step of the process from concept to successful operation.

Inside these pages, you'll find practical advice on everything from crafting your business plan and sourcing high-quality ingredients to designing your creamery layout and marketing your products effectively. We'll delve into the nuances of dairy processing, exploring the techniques and recipes that will set your creamery apart from the competition. You'll learn how to navigate the regulatory landscape, manage your finances, and overcome the inevitable challenges that come with running a small business.

But Creamery Craft is more than just a how-to manual. It's a celebration of the artistry and craftsmanship that goes into creating exceptional dairy products. It's a testament to the dedication and passion of the men and women who devote their lives to perfecting their craft and bringing joy to others through their delicious creations.

So whether you dream of churning out award-winning cheeses, scooping up creamy gelato on a hot summer day, or simply sharing the simple pleasure of a perfectly crafted glass of milk with your community, let Creamery Craft be your guide on the journey to realizing your creamery dreams.

Chapter 1:
The Creamery Industry

In this inaugural chapter, we delve into the essence of creameries, exploring the intricate dynamics that make this industry both fascinating and rewarding. From understanding the fundamentals of the creamery business to unraveling the appeal of artisanal dairy products, we'll uncover the market trends and opportunities that await aspiring creamery owners.

Understanding the Creamery Business

Creameries serve as the heartbeat of the dairy industry, where the magic of transforming fresh milk into an array of delectable dairy products comes to life. From creamy cheeses and tangy yogurts to indulgent ice creams and velvety butters, creameries are the epicenters of craftsmanship, quality, and innovation. Whether they're small-scale artisanal operations nestled in quaint countryside locales or sprawling production facilities churning out mass quantities of dairy delights, creameries hold a special place in the hearts and palates of consumers worldwide.

At the core of every creamery is a commitment to excellence, driven by a passion for preserving tradition while embracing innovation. Each product that emerges from a creamery reflects not only the skill and expertise of its makers but also a dedication to sourcing the finest ingredients and employing time-honored techniques to achieve unparalleled flavor and texture.

To truly understand the creamery business, one must delve into the intricacies of dairy processing. Processes such as pasteurization, homogenization, and fermentation are integral to transforming raw milk into the diverse range of dairy products that grace our tables and tantalize our taste buds. Pasteurization, the process of heating milk to eliminate harmful bacteria while preserving its nutritional integrity, ensures the safety and quality of dairy products. Homogenization, on the other hand, breaks down fat globules in milk to create a uniform texture, resulting in smooth and creamy products. And fermentation, a natural process facilitated by beneficial bacteria, gives rise to tangy yogurts and flavorful cheeses, imbuing them with distinctive character and complexity.

However, navigating the regulatory landscape governing the creamery business is equally crucial for success in this industry. From obtaining permits and licenses to adhering to labeling requirements and food safety standards, aspiring creamery owners must familiarize themselves with the legal framework that governs their operations. Compliance with regulations ensures consumer safety, protects brand integrity, and fosters trust and confidence in the products they produce.

Creameries are more than just facilities for dairy processing—they are bastions of tradition, innovation, and quality craftsmanship. Aspiring creamery owners must not only master the art and science of dairy processing but also navigate the regulatory complexities of the industry. With dedication, passion, and a commitment to excellence, creameries can continue to delight consumers and carve out a niche in the competitive dairy market for generations to come.

The Appeal of Artisanal Dairy Products
In today's world, where mass production and uniformity often dominate, artisanal dairy products stand out as a breath of fresh air. These carefully crafted delights are made with precision and passion, offering a taste experience that is truly unique. Whether it's the complex flavors of aged cheeses or the creamy texture of small-batch ice creams, artisanal dairy products represent the pinnacle of culinary craftsmanship.

What makes artisanal dairy products so special goes beyond just their exceptional taste. Each product tells a story, reflecting the dedication of skilled artisans, the quality of locally sourced ingredients, and the time-honored traditions that have been passed down through generations. With every bite or spoonful, consumers are transported to a place where craftsmanship and authenticity reign supreme.

As more people seek out foods that are not only delicious but also sustainable and authentic, artisanal dairy products have become increasingly popular. Unlike mass-produced items, which often sacrifice flavor for efficiency, artisanal products celebrate the diversity of local ingredients and the artistry of small-scale production. They offer a connection to the land, the animals, and the artisans who pour their hearts into creating these culinary treasures.

In essence, artisanal dairy products are more than just food— they're a celebration of tradition, quality, and community. They bring people together, foster a deeper appreciation for the culinary arts, and remind us of the rich heritage behind every bite. As the demand for locally sourced, sustainable foods continues to grow, artisanal dairy products will undoubtedly remain a beloved choice for discerning consumers who value authenticity and flavor above all else.

Market Trends and Opportunities

The dairy industry is in a constant state of flux, influenced by changing consumer preferences, technological advancements, and global market trends. Today, consumers are more discerning than ever, prioritizing freshness, transparency, and sustainability when it comes to choosing dairy products. This shift in consumer behavior has created a fertile ground for small-scale creameries to flourish, as they are uniquely positioned to offer niche products tailored to the preferences of their local communities.

Moreover, the emergence of e-commerce and direct-to-consumer sales channels has democratized access to artisanal dairy products, breaking down geographical barriers and allowing creameries to reach a wider audience. Whether through subscription services, online marketplaces, or social media platforms, creameries now have unprecedented opportunities to connect directly with consumers, bypassing traditional retail channels and fostering closer relationships with their customer base.

In this dynamic and ever-changing market landscape, aspiring creamery owners are presented with a plethora of opportunities to innovate and differentiate themselves. Whether by tapping into the growing demand for organic, grass-fed dairy products, experimenting with unique flavor combinations, or embracing sustainable production practices, there are countless avenues for creameries to carve out their niche and establish a successful business.

The key lies in understanding the evolving needs and preferences of consumers, staying abreast of industry trends and technological advancements, and embracing a spirit of creativity and entrepreneurship. By staying agile, responsive, and customer-focused, creameries can position themselves for success in an increasingly competitive market, while simultaneously contributing to the diversification and enrichment of the dairy industry as a whole.

As we embark on this journey into the world of creameries, let us embrace the rich tapestry of flavors, traditions, and entrepreneurial spirit that define this vibrant industry. From dairy enthusiasts to aspiring entrepreneurs, may this exploration ignite a passion for crafting exceptional dairy products and inspire the pursuit of creamery dreams.

Chapter 2:
Planning Your Creamery

Before diving into the intricate details of setting up your creamery, it's essential to lay a strong foundation through meticulous planning. In this chapter, we'll explore the crucial steps involved in planning your creamery, from defining your vision and mission to developing your creamery business plan then to navigating legal and regulatory considerations.

Defining Your Vision and Mission

Every thriving creamery starts with a defined vision and mission statement that encapsulates the fundamental values and goals of the business. It's crucial to take a step back and contemplate your aspirations, objectives, and the distinct value proposition that distinguishes your creamery. Are you driven by a desire to uphold time-honored dairy-making practices? Or perhaps you're motivated to push the boundaries of the industry with inventive flavor profiles? Clearly articulate your vision and mission, as they will act as guiding principles guiding your creamery journey.

Conducting Market Research

Market research serves as the foundation of any prosperous business endeavor, offering invaluable insights into consumer behaviors, market dynamics, and competitive landscapes. Begin by pinpointing your target market demographics, encompassing factors like age, income levels, and dietary inclinations. Analyze the strengths, weaknesses, and market positions of existing competitors, both on a local and regional scale.

By conducting thorough market research, you can gain a deeper understanding of the needs and preferences of your target audience, allowing you to tailor your products and marketing strategies accordingly. Identifying gaps in the market or areas where competitors may be underserving consumers can also present opportunities for differentiation and innovation.

In addition to studying consumer demographics and competitor analysis, it's essential to keep a finger on the pulse of industry trends. For instance, the rising popularity of plant-based dairy alternatives presents both challenges and opportunities for traditional dairy producers. By staying informed about these trends, you can proactively adapt your product offerings and business strategies to meet evolving consumer demands.

Market research is an ongoing process that should continue throughout the life of your creamery business. Regularly monitoring consumer preferences, market dynamics, and competitive activities will enable you to stay agile and responsive in a constantly changing business environment. Armed with the insights gleaned from market research, you can make informed decisions that drive the success and growth of your creamery venture.

Writing a Business Plan

A meticulously crafted business plan acts as a guiding framework for your creamery, mapping out your goals, approaches, and financial expectations. It starts by delineating your creamery concept, encompassing details such as your product lineup, production methodologies, and distribution channels. This section sets the foundation for your entire operation, outlining the essence of what makes your creamery unique and appealing to consumers.

Following the conceptualization of your creamery, a comprehensive analysis of your target market, competitors, and pricing strategies is imperative. Understanding the demographics and preferences of your potential customers allows you to tailor your offerings to meet their needs effectively. Concurrently, examining the strengths and weaknesses of your competitors provides valuable insights that can inform your differentiation strategies and market positioning. Moreover, establishing competitive pricing strategies ensures that your products remain attractive and viable within the marketplace.

Moving forward, your business plan should delineate your marketing and sales tactics, outlining strategies for branding, advertising, and promotional activities. Effective marketing initiatives are essential for building brand awareness, attracting customers, and fostering loyalty. Whether through traditional advertising channels or digital marketing campaigns, a well-defined marketing plan ensures that your creamery gains visibility and resonates with your target audience.

Finally, a comprehensive financial plan is vital for ensuring the financial viability and sustainability of your creamery. This entails detailing start-up costs, revenue forecasts, and profit margins, allowing you to anticipate expenses and set realistic financial goals. By meticulously analyzing the financial aspects of your business, you can identify potential challenges and opportunities, thereby facilitating informed decision-making and resource allocation.

It's crucial to remember that a business plan is not a static document but rather a dynamic tool that evolves alongside your creamery's growth and changing market conditions. Regularly revisiting and updating your business plan enables you to adapt to new challenges, capitalize on emerging opportunities, and maintain alignment with your overarching business objectives. In essence, a well-crafted business plan serves as a roadmap for success, guiding your creamery towards achieving its full potential in the competitive dairy industry.

Legal and Regulatory Considerations

Navigating the legal and regulatory terrain is paramount when initiating a creamery, guaranteeing adherence to local, state, and federal regulations overseeing food production and safety. Commencing this journey involves several key steps to ensure compliance and mitigate risks.

First and foremost, registering your business entity is essential, establishing your creamery as a legal entity recognized by the government. Depending on your jurisdiction, this may involve registering as a sole proprietorship, partnership, limited liability company (LLC), or corporation. Additionally, securing any required licenses or permits for dairy processing is imperative. These permits vary based on location and may include health permits, food processing licenses, and dairy plant permits.

Next, familiarizing yourself with food safety regulations is crucial to maintain the integrity and safety of your products. This entails understanding sanitation standards, which dictate the cleanliness and hygiene practices necessary for food production facilities. Labeling requirements must also be adhered to, ensuring that your products are accurately labeled with information such as ingredients, nutritional content, and allergen warnings. Moreover, familiarize yourself with product testing protocols, which may involve regular microbial testing to ensure the safety and quality of your dairy products.

In addition to regulatory compliance, it's prudent to consider liability insurance to safeguard your creamery against potential risks and liabilities. Liability insurance provides financial protection in the event of lawsuits, property damage, or accidents that may occur on your premises. By obtaining appropriate insurance coverage, you can mitigate the financial impact of unforeseen events and protect the long-term viability of your business.

Seeking guidance from legal and regulatory experts is advisable to ensure full compliance with all relevant laws and regulations. These professionals can offer valuable insights and guidance, helping you navigate complex legal requirements and avoid potential pitfalls. Consulting with legal experts early in the process can help identify any regulatory hurdles or challenges that may arise, allowing you to address them proactively and minimize legal risks.

Navigating the legal and regulatory landscape is a critical aspect of launching a creamery. By registering your business entity, obtaining necessary licenses and permits, adhering to food safety regulations, securing liability insurance, and seeking expert guidance, you can ensure compliance and mitigate potential legal challenges, setting the stage for a successful and sustainable creamery operation.

By meticulously planning every aspect of your creamery, from defining your vision and conducting market research to writing a comprehensive business plan and addressing legal considerations, you lay the groundwork for a successful and sustainable venture. Embrace the planning process as an opportunity to clarify your goals, identify opportunities, and mitigate risks, setting the stage for the exciting journey ahead.

Chapter 3:
Location, Equipment, and Layout

The success of a creamery often hinges on strategic decisions regarding its location, the selection of appropriate equipment, and the design of an efficient layout. In this chapter, we'll delve into the critical considerations involved in choosing the right location for your creamery, selecting suitable equipment, and designing an optimized layout to support your production processes.

Selecting an Ideal Location

Selecting the perfect location for your creamery is crucial, as it can have a profound impact on various aspects of your business, including efficiency, accessibility, and overall success. There are several factors to take into account when choosing a location:

1. Proximity to Dairy Sources: One of the primary considerations is the proximity to dairy sources for a fresh and reliable milk supply. Being close to dairy farms ensures a steady and high-quality source of milk, which is essential for producing top-notch dairy products.

2. Access to Transportation Networks: Accessibility to transportation networks is vital for efficient distribution of your products. Ensure that your chosen location provides easy access to major roads, highways, or railways, facilitating the transportation of your goods to suppliers and customers.

3. Visibility in the Local Community: The visibility of your creamery in the local community can significantly impact your brand awareness and customer footfall. Consider choosing a location that is easily accessible and visible to potential customers, such as a busy street or commercial area.

4. Zoning Regulations: Familiarize yourself with zoning regulations in the area to ensure compliance with local laws and regulations. Certain areas may have restrictions on the types of businesses that can operate, so it's essential to verify that your creamery aligns with zoning requirements.

5. Environmental Considerations: Take environmental factors into account when selecting a location for your creamery. Ensure that the area is conducive to dairy production and does not pose any risks to food safety or environmental sustainability.

6. Potential Competition: Evaluate the level of competition in the area to gauge market saturation and assess the viability of your creamery's offerings. While some competition can indicate a thriving market, too much competition may pose challenges in standing out and attracting customers.

By carefully considering these factors and conducting thorough research, you can identify the optimal location for your creamery that maximizes operational efficiency, accessibility, and overall success. Remember to weigh the pros and cons of each potential location and choose one that aligns with your business goals and objectives.

Designing Your Creamery Layout

The layout of your creamery is integral to its success, impacting workflow efficiency, space utilization, and food safety. Crafting a well-thought-out layout is essential for optimizing operations and ensuring the highest standards of sanitation. Here's how to design an effective layout:

1. Develop a Comprehensive Floor Plan: Start by creating a detailed floor plan that delineates the different production areas within your creamery. This plan should include designated zones for

receiving raw materials, processing, packaging, and storage of finished products. Mapping out these areas allows for better organization and flow of operations.

2. Segregate Production Areas: To minimize the risk of cross-contamination, it's crucial to segregate production areas based on their functions. Separate zones should be designated for handling raw milk, pasteurization, and storage of finished products. This segregation helps maintain product integrity and ensures compliance with food safety standards.

3. Consider Workflow Patterns: When designing the layout, consider the workflow patterns of your production process. Arrange equipment and workstations in a logical sequence to streamline operations and minimize unnecessary movement. This optimization of workflow patterns enhances efficiency and productivity within the creamery.

4. Optimize Equipment Placement: Strategic placement of equipment is key to maximizing space utilization and workflow efficiency. Position machinery and workstations in close proximity to minimize downtime and facilitate smooth transitions between production stages. Additionally, ensure adequate space around equipment for maintenance and cleaning purposes.

5. Prioritize Sanitation and Hygiene: Food safety and sanitation should be top priorities when designing your creamery layout. Incorporate features such as easy-to-clean surfaces, drainage systems, and designated handwashing stations to maintain a hygienic environment. Consider materials that are resistant to moisture and corrosion to minimize the risk of contamination.

6. Enhance Ergonomics: Create a safe and comfortable working environment for your staff by considering ergonomic factors in the

layout design. Arrange workstations and equipment to minimize strain and fatigue, ensuring that employees can perform their tasks efficiently and without discomfort.

By carefully planning the layout of your creamery, you can optimize workflow efficiency, maximize space utilization, and uphold the highest standards of food safety and sanitation. Investing time and effort into designing a well-organized and ergonomic layout will contribute to the success and longevity of your creamery operation.

Choosing Equipment and Machinery

Selecting the right equipment and machinery is essential for the seamless operation of your creamery, covering tasks from milk processing and pasteurization to packaging and distribution. Here's a step-by-step guide to help you choose the most suitable equipment:

1. Assess Production Needs: Begin by evaluating your production requirements based on the types of dairy products you plan to manufacture and the anticipated production volumes. This assessment will help determine the capacity and capabilities required to meet current demand and accommodate future growth.

2. Invest in Quality Equipment: Prioritize investing in high-quality, durable equipment sourced from reputable manufacturers known for their reliability and adherence to industry standards. Quality equipment not only ensures consistent product quality but also minimizes the risk of breakdowns and downtime.

3. Consider Needed Equipment: Depending on the scale and scope of your creamery operations, you may need a range of equipment including but not limited to:

- Milk Pasteurization Equipment: Essential for heating milk to eliminate harmful bacteria while preserving its nutritional value.
- Cheese Vat and Press: Used for curd formation, pressing, and shaping of cheese varieties.
- Yogurt Fermentation Tanks: Required for fermenting milk with active cultures to produce yogurt.
- Ice Cream Freezers: Necessary for freezing and churning ice cream mixtures to achieve desired consistency and texture.
- Packaging Machinery: Includes equipment for filling, sealing, and labeling containers for finished dairy products.
- Refrigeration Units: Vital for storing perishable dairy products at optimal temperatures to maintain freshness and quality.

4. Ensure Safety and Sanitation: Choose equipment that meets rigorous safety and sanitation standards to comply with food safety regulations and uphold product integrity. Look for features such as stainless steel construction, sanitary design principles, and easy-to-clean surfaces.

5. Evaluate Energy Efficiency: Opt for energy-efficient equipment models that minimize operating costs and reduce environmental impact. Look for energy-saving features and technologies designed to optimize energy consumption without compromising performance.

6. Factor in Maintenance and Support: Assess the maintenance requirements of the equipment, including cleaning protocols, routine inspections, and preventive maintenance schedules. Select equipment that comes with comprehensive warranties and ongoing support services to address any issues promptly and prolong the lifespan of your machinery.

By carefully considering your production needs, investing in quality equipment, prioritizing safety and sanitation, and evaluating factors such as capacity, energy efficiency, and maintenance requirements, you can ensure the efficient operation and long-term success of your creamery. Choosing the right equipment is a critical investment that lays the groundwork for producing high-quality dairy products and maintaining customer satisfaction.

Ensuring Food Safety and Compliance

Maintaining strict adherence to food safety regulations is paramount for the success and reputation of your creamery. Familiarize yourself with relevant local, state, and federal regulations governing dairy processing, including sanitation standards, pasteurization requirements, and product labeling guidelines. Implement robust food safety protocols, including regular equipment cleaning and sanitization, proper temperature control, and hygienic handling practices. Establish a Hazard Analysis and Critical Control Points (HACCP) plan to identify potential hazards and implement preventive measures to mitigate risks. Conduct regular inspections and audits to ensure compliance with regulatory requirements and uphold the highest standards of food safety and quality.

By carefully selecting an ideal location, designing an efficient creamery layout, choosing the right equipment and machinery, and ensuring rigorous food safety and compliance measures, you lay the groundwork for a successful and sustainable creamery operation. Embrace these practical considerations as essential components of building a foundation for success in the competitive dairy industry.

Chapter 4:
Sourcing Milk and Dairy Ingredients

This chapter delves into the essential elements of procuring milk and other dairy ingredients for your creamery. It covers a range of topics, from forging connections with local dairy farmers to implementing stringent quality control measures and embracing organic and sustainable practices. Sourcing ingredients is fundamental to the production of premium-quality dairy products, making it a pivotal aspect of your creamery's operations.

Establishing Relationships with Local Dairy Farmers

Establishing robust partnerships with local dairy farmers is essential for ensuring a steady and dependable source of fresh milk for your creamery. To initiate this process, begin by conducting research and reaching out to nearby dairy farms. You can explore avenues such as attending farmers' markets, networking with agricultural organizations, or joining local farming communities to connect with potential suppliers.

When engaging with dairy farmers, prioritize open communication and transparency. Discuss your creamery's production requirements, quality standards, and expectations regarding the milk supply. By fostering clear communication channels, you can ensure that both parties are aligned in terms of their needs and capabilities.

Collaborating with local dairy farmers not only benefits your creamery but also contributes to the growth and sustainability of the regional economy. Supporting local agriculture helps to bolster the livelihoods of farmers and strengthens the agricultural infrastructure of the community.

Furthermore, building partnerships with local farmers fosters a sense of community and mutual respect between producers and processors. By working together towards a common goal, you can establish lasting relationships built on trust, reliability, and shared values.

Forging strong partnerships with local dairy farmers is a strategic approach to securing a consistent and high-quality milk supply for your creamery. Through open communication, mutual support, and a commitment to sustainability, you can cultivate relationships that are mutually beneficial and contribute to the success of both your creamery and the local farming community.

Quality Control and Ingredient Selection

Ensuring the utmost quality of your dairy products requires a comprehensive approach to quality control. It begins with establishing stringent criteria for ingredient selection, prioritizing attributes like freshness, flavor, and nutritional value. By setting clear standards from the outset, you create a framework for sourcing ingredients that meet your creamery's exacting requirements.

Regular inspections and testing serve as essential checkpoints to verify the quality and safety of incoming milk and dairy ingredients. This involves conducting thorough microbial analysis, sensory evaluations to assess flavor and texture, and detailed assessments of chemical composition. These meticulous examinations help identify any deviations from quality standards early on, allowing for prompt corrective action.

Effective inventory management systems play a crucial role in maintaining quality control throughout the production process. By implementing robust tracking mechanisms, you can monitor ingredient usage, minimize waste, and ensure optimal stock levels.

This ensures that you always have the necessary ingredients on hand to meet production demands without the risk of excess or shortage.

Furthermore, developing comprehensive protocols for handling, storing, and transporting ingredients is essential to prevent contamination and spoilage. Proper handling procedures, adherence to hygiene protocols, and appropriate storage conditions are imperative to preserve the integrity of ingredients and safeguard against quality degradation.

By adhering to strict quality control measures at every stage of production, you not only uphold the freshness, purity, and flavor of your dairy products but also bolster customer confidence in your brand. Consistency in delivering superior-quality products not only fosters loyalty among customers but also strengthens your creamery's reputation as a trusted purveyor of exceptional dairy goods.

Organic and Sustainable Practices

Ensuring the utmost quality of your dairy products requires a comprehensive approach to quality control. It begins with establishing stringent criteria for ingredient selection, prioritizing attributes like freshness, flavor, and nutritional value. By setting clear standards from the outset, you create a framework for sourcing ingredients that meet your creamery's exacting requirements.

Regular inspections and testing serve as essential checkpoints to verify the quality and safety of incoming milk and dairy ingredients. This involves conducting thorough microbial analysis, sensory evaluations to assess flavor and texture, and detailed assessments of chemical composition. These meticulous examinations help identify any deviations from quality standards early on, allowing for prompt corrective action.

Effective inventory management systems play a crucial role in maintaining quality control throughout the production process. By implementing robust tracking mechanisms, you can monitor ingredient usage, minimize waste, and ensure optimal stock levels. This ensures that you always have the necessary ingredients on hand to meet production demands without the risk of excess or shortage.

Furthermore, developing comprehensive protocols for handling, storing, and transporting ingredients is essential to prevent contamination and spoilage. Proper handling procedures, adherence to hygiene protocols, and appropriate storage conditions are imperative to preserve the integrity of ingredients and safeguard against quality degradation.

By adhering to strict quality control measures at every stage of production, you not only uphold the freshness, purity, and flavor of your dairy products but also bolster customer confidence in your brand. Consistency in delivering superior-quality products not only fosters loyalty among customers but also strengthens your creamery's reputation as a trusted purveyor of exceptional dairy goods.

By establishing relationships with local dairy farmers, implementing rigorous quality control measures, and embracing organic and sustainable practices in your ingredient sourcing, you lay the foundation for producing premium-quality dairy products that resonate with consumers and reflect your values as a creamery. Embrace these principles as guiding pillars of your sourcing strategy, nurturing partnerships, ensuring quality, and promoting sustainability throughout your creamery journey.

Chapter 5:
Crafting Your Products

In this chapter, we delve into the art and science of crafting exceptional dairy products for your creamery. From developing a diverse product line to perfecting recipes and formulas, and implementing techniques for consistency and quality, mastering the craft of dairy production is essential to delighting your customers and distinguishing your creamery in the marketplace.

Developing Your Product Line

Crafting a product line that resonates with consumers is key to the success of any creamery. It allows you to cater to a wide range of tastes and preferences, ensuring that your offerings appeal to a diverse audience. Here's a detailed guide on how to develop an exceptional product line for your creamery:

Start by conducting thorough market research to understand the current trends, consumer preferences, and niche opportunities within your target market. By staying informed about the evolving dairy industry landscape, you can tailor your product offerings to meet the demands of your customers effectively.

Strike a balance between offering traditional favorites and introducing innovative creations to your product line. Traditional dairy products like aged cheeses and creamy yogurts appeal to those seeking familiar flavors, while innovative offerings such as artisanal ice creams and flavored milks cater to adventurous palates. Diversifying your product range will help you capture a broader audience and stand out in the marketplace.

Explore different product categories to showcase the versatility of your creamery. Consider offering an assortment of cheeses, ranging from mild and creamy varieties to bold and aged selections.

Delve into the world of yogurts, experimenting with different flavors, textures, and formulations. Don't forget to include indulgent treats like artisanal ice creams, rich butters, and flavored milks to round out your product portfolio.

Actively engage with your customers to gather feedback on your existing product line and gather insights for future development. Encourage customers to share their preferences, suggestions, and recommendations through surveys, tastings, and social media interactions. By listening to your customers' voices, you can gain valuable insights that inform product improvements and innovation.

Embrace a culture of experimentation and innovation to keep your product line fresh and exciting. Continuously explore new flavors, ingredients, and formats to captivate the taste buds of your customers. Collaborate with local producers, chefs, and artisans to infuse creativity and uniqueness into your offerings. By staying ahead of trends and pushing the boundaries of traditional dairy products, you can position your creamery as a pioneer in the industry.

Developing a well-curated product line requires a strategic blend of market research, innovation, and customer engagement. By offering a diverse array of dairy delights that cater to various tastes and preferences, you can establish your creamery as a destination for high-quality, artisanal dairy products that delight and inspire consumers.

Perfecting Recipes and Formulas

Mastering the art of recipe development and formulation is essential for creating exceptional dairy products that stand out in the competitive marketplace. Here's a detailed guide on how to excel in this crucial aspect of creamery operations:

Start by prioritizing the selection of high-quality ingredients that accentuate the natural flavors and textures of dairy. Source fresh milk from local farms known for their exceptional quality, and opt for premium cultures and enzymes to enhance the richness and depth of your products.

Embark on a culinary journey of experimentation by exploring a variety of recipes and formulations. Play around with ingredient ratios, processing techniques, and aging conditions to achieve the perfect balance of flavor, texture, and consistency in your dairy creations. Allow yourself the freedom to innovate and explore different flavor profiles to captivate the palates of your customers.

Engage in taste tests and sensory evaluations to gather valuable feedback on your experimental recipes. Solicit input from a diverse range of palates and preferences to gain insights into how different flavors and textures resonate with your target audience. Use this feedback to refine and optimize your recipes, ensuring that they meet the discerning expectations of your customers.

Once you've perfected your recipes, meticulously document them and establish standardized procedures for their production. This documentation serves as a valuable resource for your team, providing clear instructions on ingredient quantities, processing steps, and quality control measures. Standardizing your recipes ensures consistency and uniformity across batches, allowing you to replicate success and minimize variability in production.

By embracing the art of recipe development and formulation, you can unlock the full potential of your creamery and create dairy products that dazzle the senses and delight the taste buds of your customers. With a commitment to quality ingredients, creative experimentation, and continuous improvement, you can elevate your dairy offerings to new heights of excellence.

Techniques for Consistency and Quality

Ensuring consistency and quality in dairy product production is essential for building customer trust and loyalty. Here's a detailed exploration of techniques to achieve consistency and quality:

1. Standardized Processes: Establish standardized procedures for each stage of production, from ingredient sourcing to packaging. Clearly outline the steps, parameters, and quality control measures to be followed to ensure consistency in every batch of dairy products.

2. Quality Ingredient Sourcing: Source high-quality ingredients from reliable suppliers to maintain consistent flavor, texture, and nutritional value in your products. Establish strong relationships with trusted suppliers and conduct regular assessments to ensure ingredient quality and integrity.

3. Precise Measurement and Weighing: Use accurate measuring and weighing techniques to ensure precise ingredient proportions in recipes. Invest in quality weighing scales and measuring tools to minimize variations and maintain consistency in product formulations.

4. Temperature and Time Control: Monitor and control temperature and time parameters throughout the production process to achieve consistent results. Maintain precise temperatures during pasteurization, fermentation, and aging processes to ensure product safety and quality.

5. Quality Assurance and Testing: Implement rigorous quality assurance protocols, including regular testing and analysis of raw

materials, intermediate products, and finished goods. Conduct sensory evaluations, microbial testing, and chemical analysis to verify product quality and compliance with safety standards.

6. Training and Education: Provide comprehensive training and ongoing education for your production team to ensure adherence to quality standards and best practices. Empower employees with the knowledge and skills needed to maintain consistency and quality in every aspect of production.

7. Continuous Improvement: Foster a culture of continuous improvement by regularly evaluating and refining production processes. Solicit feedback from customers, employees, and stakeholders to identify areas for enhancement and innovation. Implementing feedback-driven improvements allows you to continually raise the bar for quality and consistency in your dairy products.

By implementing these techniques for consistency and quality, you can uphold the highest standards of excellence in your creamery's operations. Consistently delivering top-quality dairy products not only satisfies customers but also reinforces your brand's reputation for excellence and reliability in the marketplace.

By developing a diverse product line, perfecting recipes and formulas, and implementing techniques for consistency and quality, you establish your creamery as a trusted purveyor of premium dairy products that delight customers and exceed expectations. Embrace the creative process of product development, continuously seeking inspiration and innovation to push the boundaries of flavor and craftsmanship. Let your passion for dairy shine through in every batch, inviting customers to savor the artistry and dedication that goes into each delicious creation.

Chapter 6:
Packaging and Branding

Packaging and branding are essential elements in the success of your creamery. In this chapter, we explore the intricacies of designing eye-catching packaging, creating a memorable brand identity, and implementing effective marketing strategies to showcase your products to the world.

Designing Eye-Catching Packaging

Packaging serves as the first point of contact between your dairy products and potential customers, making a lasting impression and influencing purchasing decisions. Invest in visually appealing packaging designs that capture the essence of your brand and communicate the quality and uniqueness of your products.

Consider factors such as color, typography, imagery, and texture to create packaging that stands out on store shelves and resonates with your target audience. Incorporate elements of creativity and innovation to differentiate your products from competitors and spark curiosity and excitement among consumers.

Additionally, prioritize functionality and sustainability, choosing packaging materials that are durable, convenient, and environmentally friendly. Your packaging should not only attract attention but also enhance the user experience for consumers, making it easy to open, resealable, and convenient for storage and transportation.

Embrace environmentally friendly packaging solutions that minimize environmental impact and resonate with eco-conscious consumers. Opt for recyclable, biodegradable, or compostable materials to reduce waste and support sustainability initiatives.

Communicate your commitment to sustainability through transparent labeling and messaging on your packaging.

Ensure that your packaging complies with relevant regulatory requirements and industry standards for food safety and labeling. Adhere to guidelines regarding packaging materials, product information, allergen declarations, and nutritional labeling to maintain compliance and consumer trust.

Creating a Memorable Brand Identity

Your creamery's brand identity is its soul, embodying your values, personality, and commitment to customers. Here's a comprehensive guide to developing a compelling brand identity that resonates with consumers:

Craft a Captivating Brand Story: Develop a narrative that narrates the heritage, craftsmanship, and passion that go into your dairy products. Your brand story should evoke emotions and forge connections with consumers, inviting them to become part of your creamery's journey.

Create Memorable Brand Elements: Invest in a brand name, logo, and visual identity that encapsulate the unique essence of your creamery. Choose elements that convey authenticity, quality, and innovation, reflecting the aspirations and values of your brand.

Apply Consistent Branding: Ensure uniformity in your brand presentation across all touchpoints, including packaging, signage, marketing materials, and digital platforms. Consistent application of brand elements strengthens brand recognition and fosters trust among consumers.

Engage Customers Through Storytelling: Use storytelling as a powerful tool to engage and connect with your audience on a deeper level. Share stories about your creamery's origins, production process, and community involvement to humanize your brand and build authentic relationships with customers.

Foster Community Engagement: Cultivate a sense of community around your brand by actively engaging with customers and stakeholders. Participate in local events, sponsor community initiatives, and collaborate with other businesses to establish your creamery as an integral part of the community.

Utilize Social Media: Leverage social media platforms to amplify your brand presence and connect with a wider audience. Share behind-the-scenes glimpses, customer testimonials, and product updates to keep followers engaged and informed. Respond to comments and messages promptly to demonstrate your commitment to customer satisfaction.

By crafting a compelling brand story, creating memorable brand elements, maintaining consistent branding, engaging customers through storytelling, fostering community engagement, and leveraging social media, you can build a strong and enduring brand identity for your creamery. A well-defined brand identity not only differentiates your creamery in the marketplace but also fosters loyalty and affinity among consumers, driving long-term success and growth.

Marketing Your Products Effectively

Crafting an effective marketing strategy is essential for promoting your creamery and enticing customers to indulge in your dairy delights. Here are some key steps to consider:

Know Your Audience:
Understanding your target audience is crucial for tailoring your promotions effectively. Dive deep into their preferences,

demographics, and dietary habits. Are they health-conscious individuals seeking artisanal dairy products, families looking for wholesome treats, or dessert enthusiasts craving indulgent delights? Customizing your promotions to resonate with your audience's desires ensures that your efforts are well-received and appreciated.

Highlight Unique Selling Points:
Identifying what sets your creamery apart is essential for attracting customers. Whether it's your signature artisanal cheeses, farm-fresh ice creams, or sustainable sourcing practices, emphasize these unique aspects in your promotions. Highlighting what makes your creamery distinct helps you stand out from competitors and becomes the focal point of your marketing efforts.

Craft a Comprehensive Marketing Strategy:
Then proceed to formulating a comprehensive marketing plan that encompasses both traditional and digital channels. Tailor your strategy to resonate with your target audience and align with your creamery's brand identity and goals.

Leverage Digital Channels:
Harness the power of social media platforms, email marketing, and content marketing to connect with customers and showcase your dairy products. Engage with followers through captivating content, behind-the-scenes stories, and product highlights to cultivate a loyal and engaged audience.

Online Presence and Social Media Marketing
Social media is a powerful tool for showcasing your creamery's offerings and engaging with potential customers. Utilize platforms like Instagram and Facebook to visually showcase your dairy products, share behind-the-scenes glimpses of your production process, and interact with your audience. Visual storytelling

through high-quality images and videos can evoke cravings and anticipation, enticing customers to visit your creamery.

Key Strategies for Social Media Marketing:
Visual Storytelling:
Captivate your audience with mouthwatering visuals of your dairy products. Showcase the creamy textures, vibrant colors, and irresistible flavors through enticing images and videos. Visual storytelling brings your products to life and encourages customers to envision themselves savoring your creations.

Platform Selection:
Choose social media platforms that align with your creamery's brand identity and target audience. Instagram is ideal for showcasing visually appealing content, while Facebook allows for deeper engagement and interaction. Tailor your content strategy to each platform to maximize engagement and reach.

Consistent Branding:
Maintain a cohesive brand identity across all your social media channels. Ensure that your profile pictures, cover photos, and captions reflect the ambiance and values of your creamery. Consistent branding helps reinforce your brand image and fosters recognition among your audience.

Engaging Content:
Create content that sparks conversations and interactions. Share stories about your dairy products, introduce the farmers and artisans behind your ingredients, and provide insights into your production process. Engage your audience with interactive features like polls, quizzes, and behind-the-scenes videos.

User-Generated Content:

Encourage your customers to share their experiences with your dairy products on social media. User-generated content serves as authentic testimonials and builds a sense of community around your brand. Reposting customer photos and reviews can further amplify your online presence.

Hashtags and Trends:
Incorporate relevant hashtags and trends into your posts to increase visibility and reach. Research popular food-related hashtags and leverage trending topics to expand your audience and attract new followers.

Storytelling:
Craft compelling captions that go beyond product descriptions. Share anecdotes about the inspiration behind your dairy products, the craftsmanship involved in their creation, and the passion driving your team. Storytelling creates an emotional connection with your audience and enhances their appreciation for your brand.

Engagement and Response:
Interact with your audience by responding to comments, messages, and mentions promptly. Show appreciation for their feedback, questions, and suggestions to foster a sense of community and customer loyalty.

Promotions and Offers:
Use your social media platforms to promote special events, seasonal flavors, and exclusive discounts. Create excitement and urgency around your promotions to encourage customers to visit your creamery and indulge in your dairy delights.

Analysis and Adaptation:

Regularly analyze your social media metrics to gain insights into what resonates most with your audience. Use this data to refine your content strategy, optimize engagement, and drive business results. Adapt your approach based on feedback and performance metrics to ensure ongoing success in your social media marketing efforts.

Social media marketing for creameries is a dynamic and creative endeavor that allows you to connect with customers, showcase your products, and build a loyal following. By leveraging the power of social media platforms to tell your brand story, engage with your audience, and share the magic of your dairy creations, you can turn online interactions into real-world experiences that delight and satisfy customers.

Collaborations and Partnerships
Forming local partnerships and collaborations can add depth and authenticity to your creamery's promotional endeavors. By teaming up with businesses that share similar values, aesthetics, or target audiences, you can expand your reach and build a resilient community network. These collaborations not only enhance your brand's credibility but also infuse your promotions with a genuine sense of local pride.

Strategies for Local Partnerships and Collaborations:

1. Align with Complementary Businesses:
Identify businesses that complement your creamery's offerings and share similar values. This could include local farms, bakeries, coffee shops, or artisanal food producers. Collaborating with these businesses allows you to create partnerships that benefit both parties and resonate with your shared customer base.

2. Craft Joint Promotions:

Develop promotions that highlight the synergy between your creamery and your partnering businesses. This could involve creating special menu items featuring local ingredients, hosting collaborative tasting events, or offering bundled packages that showcase products from both businesses.

3. Shared Social Media Campaigns:
Collaborate on social media content with your partners to reach a wider audience. Share each other's posts, tag one another in relevant content, and use common hashtags to increase visibility and engagement. By leveraging each other's social media presence, you can amplify the impact of your promotional efforts.

4. Host Collaborative Events:
Organize events that showcase the offerings of both your creamery and your partners. This could include food and beverage pairings, cooking workshops, or themed tasting events. Collaborative events provide a unique and memorable experience for customers while highlighting the diversity of local businesses.

5. Cross-Promotions:
Encourage customers to explore both your creamery and your partner's business by offering incentives such as discounts or special offers. For example, customers who purchase a pint of ice cream from your creamery could receive a coupon for a discount at the partnering coffee shop.

6. Share Resources:
Maximize your promotional efforts by sharing resources with your partners. This could include sharing mailing lists, co-hosting promotional events, or pooling marketing budgets for joint advertising campaigns. By working together, you can achieve greater visibility and impact than you would on your own.

7. Community Engagement:
Get involved in local community events and initiatives alongside your partners. This could include participating in farmers' markets, street fairs, or charity fundraisers together. By demonstrating your commitment to the community, you can strengthen relationships with customers and fellow businesses alike.

Collaborating with local businesses offers a valuable opportunity to connect with your community and enhance your creamery's visibility and reputation. By leveraging each other's strengths and resources, you can create memorable experiences for customers while fostering a sense of unity and support within the local business community.

Loyalty Programs

Developing a comprehensive loyalty program for your creamery is a strategic initiative aimed at fostering customer loyalty and cultivating a sense of appreciation and connection with your clientele. This program involves offering exclusive rewards and benefits to returning customers as a token of acknowledgment for their continued support.

A well-designed loyalty program typically consists of tiered membership levels, each offering progressively enticing perks and rewards. For example, you could have tiers like "Silver," "Gold," and "Platinum," with each level unlocking a range of benefits.

1. Tiered Membership Levels:
   - Silver: This entry-level tier might offer perks like a small discount on the next purchase or a free topping with each ice cream purchase.
   - Gold: Customers in the Gold tier could receive more significant benefits, such as a larger discount on their purchases or a free scoop of ice cream on their birthday.

- Platinum: The highest-tier Platinum members could enjoy exclusive privileges, such as priority access to new flavors or special members-only events.

By segmenting your customer base into tiers, you can tailor rewards to align with individual preferences and spending habits, thereby demonstrating a deep understanding of their needs.

2. Personalized Rewards:
   - Collect and analyze data on customer preferences and behaviors to personalize rewards and offers. For example, you could offer discounts on their favorite flavors or provide bonus points for referrals.
   - Use customer feedback and purchase history to tailor promotions and incentives to each customer's interests and tastes, making them feel valued and appreciated.

3. Enhanced Customer Engagement:
   - Implementing a loyalty program encourages customers to return to your creamery to earn rewards, thus increasing customer retention and lifetime value.
   - Engage with customers through targeted communications and promotions to keep them informed about new flavors, promotions, and special events. This ongoing engagement helps to strengthen the bond between your creamery and its loyal customers.

4. Word-of-Mouth Marketing:
   - Satisfied customers who benefit from your loyalty program are more likely to share their positive experiences with friends and family, leading to word-of-mouth referrals and increased brand awareness.
   - Encourage customers to refer their friends to your creamery by offering referral bonuses or discounts for both the referrer and the

new customer. This incentivizes existing customers to spread the word about your business.

5. Analysis and Optimization:
   - Regularly review and analyze data on loyalty program performance to identify trends and opportunities for improvement.
   - Use insights from customer feedback and redemption patterns to refine your program and optimize rewards for maximum impact.

In summary, a well-executed loyalty program not only strengthens customer relationships and boosts retention but also serves as a powerful marketing tool for driving repeat business and attracting new customers to your creamery. By offering personalized rewards, enhancing customer engagement, and continually refining your program based on feedback and data, you can create a rewarding experience that keeps customers coming back for more.

By designing eye-catching packaging, creating a memorable brand identity, and implementing effective marketing strategies, you position your creamery for success in a competitive market landscape. Embrace the opportunity to showcase the quality, craftsmanship, and passion that define your dairy products, inviting customers to experience the joy and satisfaction of indulging in your delicious creations.

Chapter 7:
Operations and Management

In this chapter, we delve into the critical aspects of running and managing the day-to-day operations of your creamery. From staffing considerations to inventory management and establishing standard operating procedures, effective operations and management are essential for ensuring efficiency, consistency, and success in your creamery venture.

Staffing Your Creamery

Staffing your creamery with the right team is essential for ensuring smooth operations and delivering high-quality products and services. Here's a detailed guide on how to effectively staff your creamery:

1. Define Roles and Responsibilities: Defining roles and responsibilities is essential for ensuring smooth operations and effective teamwork within your creamery. By clearly outlining the functions and duties of each position, you provide clarity and direction for your team members. Here's how you can define roles and responsibilities in your creamery:

Identify Necessary Positions: Start by identifying the key positions required to run your creamery efficiently. This may include roles such as production staff, packaging specialists, sales associates, customer service representatives, administrative personnel, and management positions.

Determine Specific Tasks and Duties: Once you've identified the necessary positions, outline the specific tasks and responsibilities associated with each role. For example:
  - Production Staff: Responsibilities may include milk processing, cheese making, yogurt production, and other dairy-related tasks.

- Packaging Specialists: Duties may involve packaging finished products, labeling, ensuring product quality and presentation, and maintaining inventory levels of packaging materials.
- Sales Associates: Tasks may include assisting customers, processing orders, handling inquiries, and promoting products.
- Administrative Personnel: Responsibilities may include managing schedules, handling paperwork, coordinating shipments, managing finances, and overseeing office operations.
- Management Positions: Duties may involve strategic planning, decision-making, staff supervision, budget management, and ensuring compliance with regulations.

2. Hire Skilled and Passionate Individuals: Seek out individuals who are not only skilled and experienced but also passionate about the dairy industry and committed to upholding your creamery's values and standards. Look for candidates with relevant experience in food production, dairy processing, customer service, and other relevant fields. Consider conducting thorough interviews and assessments to ensure a good fit for your team.

3. Provide Training and Development: Invest in training and development programs to equip your staff with the knowledge, skills, and tools needed to excel in their roles. Offer comprehensive training on dairy production techniques, food safety protocols, equipment operation, customer service best practices, and other relevant areas. Encourage ongoing learning and professional development opportunities to foster growth and advancement within your creamery.

4. Foster a Positive Work Environment: Create a positive and supportive work environment that fosters teamwork, collaboration, and mutual respect among your staff. Encourage open communication, recognize and reward employee contributions, and provide opportunities for feedback and

dialogue. A positive work culture enhances employee satisfaction and morale, leading to increased productivity and job satisfaction.

5. Prioritize Safety and Compliance: Ensure that your creamery adheres to strict safety and compliance standards to protect the well-being of your staff and customers. Implement safety protocols, provide proper training on equipment usage and handling hazardous materials, and maintain a clean and sanitary work environment. Stay updated on relevant regulations and requirements to ensure full compliance with industry standards.

6. Foster a Culture of Excellence: Strive for excellence in every aspect of your creamery's operations and instill a culture of continuous improvement among your staff. Set high standards for product quality, customer service, and efficiency, and empower your team to innovate and contribute to the success of the creamery. Encourage feedback, embrace new ideas, and celebrate achievements to inspire a sense of pride and ownership among your staff.

By carefully staffing your creamery with skilled, passionate individuals, providing comprehensive training and development, fostering a positive work environment, prioritizing safety and compliance, and promoting a culture of excellence, you can build a strong and dedicated team that drives the success of your creamery. A well-trained and motivated staff is essential for delivering exceptional products and services and building long-term relationships with customers.

Inventory Management and Supply Chain
Inventory management and supply chain operations are critical aspects of running a successful creamery. Here's a detailed look at how to effectively manage your inventory and optimize your supply chain:

Effective inventory management is essential for ensuring that your creamery has the right amount of ingredients, packaging materials, and finished products on hand to meet customer demand while minimizing waste and excess inventory. It involves accurately tracking inventory levels, forecasting demand, and implementing efficient replenishment processes.

One key aspect of inventory management is maintaining optimal stock levels to prevent stockouts or overstock situations. By closely monitoring inventory levels and demand patterns, you can identify trends and adjust your ordering and production schedules accordingly to avoid shortages or excess inventory buildup.

Additionally, implementing inventory management software or systems can streamline the tracking and management of inventory data, providing real-time visibility into stock levels, order status, and inventory turnover rates. This enables more accurate forecasting, better decision-making, and improved inventory control.

Effective supply chain management is essential for ensuring the timely and cost-effective delivery of raw materials, packaging supplies, and other inputs needed for production. It involves sourcing materials from reliable suppliers, managing supplier relationships, and optimizing transportation and logistics processes.

One key aspect of supply chain management is selecting and managing suppliers who can consistently deliver quality materials on time and at competitive prices. Building strong relationships with suppliers and negotiating favorable terms can help minimize supply chain disruptions and ensure a reliable source of inputs for your creamery.

Additionally, optimizing transportation and logistics processes can help reduce lead times, lower transportation costs, and improve overall supply chain efficiency. This may involve consolidating shipments, optimizing delivery routes, and using technology solutions such as GPS tracking and route optimization software.

Overall, effective inventory management and supply chain operations are essential for ensuring the smooth and efficient operation of your creamery. By closely monitoring inventory levels, optimizing replenishment processes, selecting reliable suppliers, and streamlining transportation and logistics, you can minimize costs, reduce waste, and improve customer satisfaction.

Establishing Standard Operating Procedures

Establishing Standard Operating Procedures (SOPs) is crucial for maintaining consistency, efficiency, and quality in the operations of your creamery. Here's a detailed guide on how to develop and implement SOPs:

1. Identify Key Processes: Begin by identifying the key processes and tasks involved in running your creamery, including milk processing, cheese making, packaging, sanitation, and equipment maintenance. Break down each process into specific steps and tasks to create a comprehensive list of activities.

2. Document Procedures: Document detailed procedures for each process, outlining the steps to be followed, the sequence of operations, and the responsibilities of each team member. Include clear instructions, safety guidelines, and quality control measures to ensure that tasks are performed consistently and accurately.

3. Standardize Workflows: Standardize workflows and best practices to streamline operations and minimize variability. Define

standardized methods for handling ingredients, operating equipment, performing quality checks, and addressing common challenges or issues that may arise during production.

4. Train Employees: Provide comprehensive training to your staff on the SOPs relevant to their roles and responsibilities. Ensure that employees understand the procedures, safety protocols, and quality standards outlined in the SOPs through hands-on training, demonstrations, and written materials. Offer ongoing training and refresher courses to reinforce learning and address any gaps in knowledge or skills.

5. Implement Quality Control Measures: Integrate quality control measures into your SOPs to ensure that products meet the highest standards of quality and safety. Include protocols for inspecting raw materials, monitoring production processes, conducting product testing, and addressing non-conformities or deviations from established standards.

6. Review and Update Regularly: Regularly review and update your SOPs to reflect changes in processes, equipment, regulations, or best practices. Solicit feedback from employees, supervisors, and stakeholders to identify areas for improvement and incorporate any necessary revisions or enhancements into the SOPs.

7. Monitor Compliance: Monitor compliance with SOPs through regular audits, inspections, and performance evaluations. Ensure that employees are following procedures correctly and consistently, and address any deviations or non-compliance promptly through corrective actions or retraining efforts.

8. Foster a Culture of Continuous Improvement: Foster a culture of continuous improvement within your creamery by encouraging employees to suggest ideas for optimizing processes, enhancing

efficiency, and improving quality. Empower employees to participate in problem-solving and decision-making processes, and recognize and reward contributions to process improvement initiatives.

By establishing standardized operating procedures, training employees effectively, implementing quality control measures, and fostering a culture of continuous improvement, you can ensure that your creamery operates efficiently, consistently, and safely, producing high-quality dairy products that meet customer expectations.

By staffing your creamery with a dedicated and skilled team, implementing effective inventory management practices, and establishing standard operating procedures, you create a solid foundation for success in the competitive dairy industry. Embrace the opportunity to optimize your operations and management processes, continuously seeking opportunities for improvement and innovation to enhance efficiency, quality, and customer satisfaction in your creamery venture.

Chapter 8:
Financial Management

In this chapter, we delve into the crucial aspects of financial management for your creamery business. From estimating start-up costs to creating a budget and financial forecast, and developing pricing strategies to maximize profit margins, effective financial management is essential for the long-term success and sustainability of your creamery.

Estimating Start-up Costs

Before launching your creamery, it's essential to have a clear understanding of the initial investment required to get your business off the ground. Here's a detailed guide on how to estimate the initial costs involved in starting your creamery:

Equipment and Machinery: Begin by identifying the equipment and machinery needed for milk processing, cheese making, packaging, and other operations. Research suppliers, obtain quotes, and calculate the cost of purchasing or leasing essential equipment such as pasteurizers, cheese vats, refrigeration units, packaging machines, and storage tanks.

Facility and Renovations: Consider the cost of securing a suitable facility for your creamery, including lease or purchase costs, rent deposits, and any necessary renovations or improvements to meet regulatory requirements and operational needs. Factor in expenses such as construction, plumbing, electrical work, flooring, and ventilation systems.

Licensing and Permits: Research the licensing and permit requirements for operating a creamery in your area, including health permits, food processing licenses, dairy permits, and zoning permits. Estimate the costs associated with obtaining these permits, including application fees, inspections, and regulatory compliance expenses.

Raw Materials and Ingredients: Estimate the initial cost of purchasing raw materials and ingredients needed for production, such as milk, cultures, enzymes, rennet, flavorings, and packaging materials. Research suppliers, obtain price quotes, and calculate the cost of stocking inventory to support your production needs.

Labor Costs: Estimate the labor costs associated with hiring and training employees to staff your creamery. Consider factors such as wages, salaries, benefits, payroll taxes, and employee training expenses. Determine the number of staff members needed to operate your creamery efficiently and factor in their compensation into your startup budget.

Marketing and Branding: Allocate funds for marketing and branding initiatives to promote your creamery and attract customers. Estimate the cost of designing a logo, creating branding materials, developing a website, printing marketing materials, and launching advertising campaigns. Consider expenses such as social media marketing, website development, photography, and promotional events.

Utilities and Operating Expenses: Estimate the ongoing operational expenses associated with running your creamery, including utilities such as electricity, water, gas, and internet services. Factor in expenses such as insurance premiums, rent or mortgage payments, property taxes, equipment maintenance, and cleaning supplies.

Contingency Fund: Set aside a contingency fund to cover unexpected expenses or emergencies that may arise during the startup phase of your creamery. Aim to allocate around 10-20% of your total startup budget for contingency purposes to mitigate financial risks and ensure you have sufficient funds to address unforeseen challenges.

By carefully estimating your startup costs and budgeting for each aspect of launching your creamery, you can develop a realistic financial plan and secure the necessary funding to get your business off the ground successfully. Conduct thorough research, seek multiple quotes, and consult with industry experts to ensure that your estimates are accurate and comprehensive.

Creating a Budget and Financial Forecast

Developing a detailed budget and financial forecast is essential for managing your creamery's finances effectively and planning for future growth and profitability. Here's a detailed guide on how to develop a budget and financial forecast for your creamery:

1. Revenue Projections: Begin by estimating your creamery's potential revenue streams based on sales projections for your dairy products. Consider factors such as pricing, sales volume, market demand, and seasonality when forecasting sales. Utilize market research, competitor analysis, and industry trends to inform your revenue projections.

2. Cost of Goods Sold (COGS): Calculate the cost of goods sold (COGS) associated with producing your dairy products, including raw materials, ingredients, packaging materials, and direct labor costs. Determine the cost per unit for each product and multiply it by the projected sales volume to estimate total COGS.

3. Operating Expenses: Identify and categorize your creamery's operating expenses, including overhead costs such as rent or mortgage payments, utilities, insurance premiums, marketing expenses, administrative costs, and miscellaneous expenses.

Estimate each expense category based on historical data, industry benchmarks, and future projections.

4. Capital Expenditures: Budget for any significant capital expenditures needed to purchase equipment, machinery, or facilities for your creamery. Consider the depreciation schedule for long-term assets and factor in maintenance and repair costs to ensure accurate budgeting for capital expenditures.

5. Cash Flow Management: Develop a cash flow forecast to project your creamery's cash inflows and outflows over a specific period, typically monthly or quarterly. Estimate cash receipts from sales, investments, loans, and other sources, and deduct cash disbursements for expenses, purchases, debt repayment, and capital investments. Monitor your cash flow regularly to ensure that your creamery has sufficient liquidity to meet its financial obligations and fund its operations.

6. Profitability Analysis: Conduct a profitability analysis to assess the financial viability of your creamery and determine its potential for generating profits. Calculate key financial metrics such as gross profit margin, net profit margin, return on investment (ROI), and break-even point to evaluate the profitability of your business model and identify areas for improvement.

7. Sensitivity Analysis: Perform sensitivity analysis to assess the impact of potential changes in key variables, such as sales volume, pricing, or costs, on your creamery's financial performance. Identify potential risks and uncertainties that may affect your budget and financial forecast, and develop contingency plans to mitigate these risks effectively.

8. Review and Adjust: Regularly review and adjust your budget and financial forecast based on actual performance, changes in market

conditions, and emerging trends. Compare actual results to budgeted projections, analyze variances, and adjust your forecasts accordingly to maintain financial stability and achieve your creamery's strategic objectives.

By creating a comprehensive budget and financial forecast for your creamery, you can effectively manage your finances, make informed decisions, and optimize your business operations for long-term success. Be proactive in monitoring your creamery's financial performance, and be prepared to adapt your budget and forecast as needed to navigate changing market conditions and achieve your financial goals.

Pricing Strategies and Profit Margins

Determining the right pricing strategy is pivotal for ensuring the financial health and profitability of your creamery business. It involves a comprehensive analysis of various factors such as production costs, market demand, competitor pricing, and perceived value of your dairy products.

To begin with, a thorough examination of production costs is essential. This entails calculating the cost of goods sold (COGS) for each product, taking into account expenses like raw materials, labor, overhead, packaging, and other direct costs associated with manufacturing. Understanding these costs allows you to establish a break-even point, which is crucial for determining a baseline selling price that covers expenses and ensures profitability.

Market research plays a vital role in shaping your pricing strategy. By assessing market demand, understanding customer preferences, and analyzing competitor pricing strategies, you can gain insights into pricing dynamics within your industry. This information helps you identify opportunities for pricing optimization and differentiation in the market.

When it comes to pricing strategies, there are several approaches to consider. One common method is cost-plus pricing, where you add a markup to your production costs to determine the selling price. Alternatively, value-based pricing focuses on setting prices based on the perceived value of your products to customers, emphasizing quality, uniqueness, and benefits. Competitive pricing involves benchmarking your prices against competitors to ensure competitiveness in the market and adjusting prices accordingly.

Profit margin considerations are also paramount in pricing strategy development. Balancing the need to generate profits with the goal of offering competitive prices requires careful calculation and analysis. By setting prices that achieve desired profit margins while remaining attractive to customers, you can strike the right balance between profitability and competitiveness.

Flexibility is key in pricing strategy implementation. Market conditions, customer preferences, and competitive pressures may change over time, necessitating adjustments to pricing strategies. Continuous monitoring of market trends, sales data, and customer feedback allows you to make informed decisions and adapt your pricing approach as needed.

Moreover, offering pricing tiers or bundling options can cater to different customer segments and increase sales opportunities. Creating value-added bundles or packages that combine multiple products or offering discounts for bulk purchases can incentivize higher spending and enhance customer loyalty.

In conclusion, developing an effective pricing strategy for your creamery involves a systematic analysis of production costs, market dynamics, competitor pricing, and profit margins. By carefully considering these factors and maintaining flexibility in your approach, you can set prices that maximize profitability, drive sales, and position your creamery for success in the competitive dairy market.

By estimating start-up costs accurately, creating a comprehensive budget and financial forecast, and developing pricing strategies to maximize profit margins, you lay the foundation for financial success and sustainability in your creamery business. Embrace financial management as a strategic tool for driving growth and profitability, empowering you to make informed decisions and navigate the financial challenges and opportunities that arise in the dynamic dairy industry.

Chapter 9:
Distribution and Sales

Distribution and sales play a pivotal role in bringing your dairy products to market and reaching your target audience effectively. In this chapter, we explore the strategies and channels for distributing and selling your products, whether it's through direct-to-consumer channels, partnerships with retailers, or collaborations with restaurants and specialty food establishments.

Developing Distribution Channels

Choosing the right distribution channels is a critical aspect of successfully bringing your dairy products to consumers in a cost-effective and efficient manner. Here's an in-depth exploration of how to select the most suitable distribution channels for your creamery:

1. Assess Distribution Options: Begin by evaluating the various distribution channels available to you, considering factors such as your target market, production capacity, and business objectives. Common distribution options include direct sales, wholesale distribution, foodservice, and online sales. Each channel has its advantages and challenges, so it's essential to weigh the pros and cons based on your specific circumstances.

2. Direct Sales: Direct sales involve selling your dairy products directly to consumers through channels such as farmers' markets, on-farm stores, or your creamery's retail outlet. This approach allows you to establish a direct connection with customers, gather feedback, and retain greater control over pricing and brand presentation. However, it requires significant investment in marketing, sales, and distribution infrastructure.

3. Wholesale Distribution: Wholesale distribution involves selling your products in bulk to retailers, specialty food stores, or distributors who then sell them to end consumers. This channel offers broader market reach, access to established distribution networks, and potential volume sales. Partnering with wholesalers or distributors allows you to focus on production while leveraging their expertise in sales and distribution.

4. Foodservice: Foodservice distribution involves supplying your dairy products to restaurants, cafes, hotels, and other food establishments. This channel can be lucrative, especially if you offer specialty or artisanal products that cater to chefs and culinary professionals. Developing relationships with chefs, foodservice distributors, and culinary influencers can help you penetrate this market segment effectively.

5. Online Sales: With the rise of e-commerce, online sales have become increasingly popular for selling dairy products directly to consumers. Setting up an e-commerce platform or selling through online marketplaces allows you to reach a broader audience beyond your local market and tap into the growing demand for artisanal and specialty foods. However, online sales require investment in website development, digital marketing, and fulfillment infrastructure.

6. Identify Distributors and Partners: Once you've determined your preferred distribution channels, identify potential distributors, brokers, or wholesalers who specialize in dairy products and have existing relationships with retailers and foodservice providers in your target market. Research potential partners, attend industry trade shows, and network with industry professionals to find suitable distribution partners who align with your brand values and business goals.

7. Regional vs. National vs. International Distribution: Consider the scale and scope of your creamery operations when deciding on the geographic reach of your distribution channels. Regional distribution may be more feasible for smaller creameries with limited production capacity, while larger operations may opt for national or international distribution to reach a broader market. Evaluate the logistics, transportation costs, regulatory requirements, and market potential of each distribution option before making a decision.

8. Develop Partnerships and Negotiate Agreements: Once you've identified potential distribution partners, initiate discussions and negotiate agreements that outline the terms of the partnership, including pricing, payment terms, distribution territories, marketing support, and brand representation. Collaborate closely with your distributors to ensure reliable and cost-effective distribution of your products while maintaining control over pricing, quality, and brand integrity.

By carefully evaluating your distribution options, identifying suitable partners, and negotiating agreements that align with your business objectives, you can establish effective distribution channels for your creamery and maximize the reach and profitability of your dairy products in the marketplace.

Selling Directly to Consumers (Farmers Markets, Stores, Online)
Direct-to-consumer sales channels present a valuable opportunity for creameries to establish a direct connection with customers, cultivate brand loyalty, and maximize profit margins. Here's an in-depth exploration of how to leverage various direct-to-consumer sales channels effectively:

1. Farmers' Markets: Farmers' markets provide an ideal platform for creameries to showcase their products, interact with customers

face-to-face, and build relationships within the local community. Participating in farmers' markets allows you to offer samples, educate consumers about your dairy products, and gather feedback directly from customers. Research local farmers' markets in your area, secure vendor spots, and invest in eye-catching signage and displays to attract attention to your booth.

2. Farm Stands: Setting up a farm stand at your creamery allows you to sell dairy products directly to customers who visit your production facility. Farm stands offer a convenient and authentic shopping experience for customers, allowing them to purchase fresh products straight from the source. Create an inviting and welcoming environment at your farm stand, and consider offering additional attractions such as farm tours or tastings to enhance the customer experience.

3. On-Farm Retail: Establishing an on-farm retail store provides a permanent retail space for customers to purchase your dairy products. Design your retail space to reflect your creamery's brand aesthetic and values, and stock it with a diverse selection of products to cater to different tastes and preferences. Consider offering value-added services such as cheese tasting events, workshops, or educational tours to engage customers and drive foot traffic to your retail location.

4. Pop-Up Events: Organizing pop-up events at local venues or community gatherings offers a temporary but impactful way to promote your dairy products and reach new customers. Partner with local businesses, organizations, or event organizers to host pop-up events at festivals, fairs, or food-related gatherings. Create buzz around your pop-up events through social media marketing, email newsletters, and word-of-mouth advertising to attract attendees and drive sales.

5. Online Sales Platforms: Embrace online sales platforms to expand your reach beyond your local market and tap into a broader audience of potential customers. Develop a user-friendly and visually appealing website for your creamery, where customers can browse your product offerings, place orders, and learn more about your brand story. Alternatively, leverage third-party e-commerce platforms such as Etsy, Shopify, or Amazon to reach a wider audience and benefit from their existing customer base.

6. Invest in Online Presence: Invest in professional website design, high-quality product photography, and secure payment processing to create a seamless online shopping experience for customers. Ensure that your website is mobile-responsive and optimized for search engines to improve visibility and attract organic traffic. Implement customer-friendly features such as product reviews, wishlists, and personalized recommendations to enhance the shopping experience and encourage repeat purchases.

7. Marketing and Promotions: Implement marketing strategies such as promotions, discounts, and loyalty programs to incentivize repeat purchases and foster customer loyalty in your direct-to-consumer sales channels. Offer special deals or exclusive discounts for first-time customers, and reward loyal customers with perks such as free samples, birthday discounts, or referral rewards. Leverage email marketing, social media campaigns, and targeted advertising to promote your direct-to-consumer sales channels and drive traffic to your online and offline retail outlets.

By exploring and investing in a diverse range of direct-to-consumer sales channels, creameries can effectively engage with customers, build brand loyalty, and maximize profit margins while offering a unique and personalized shopping experience.

Partnering with Restaurants and Specialty Food Retailers

Collaborating with restaurants and specialty food retailers offers an excellent opportunity for creameries to expand their market reach and introduce their dairy products to a wider audience in diverse culinary settings. To begin, it's essential to identify potential partners that align with your creamery's brand values, target demographic, and product offerings. Look for gourmet cheese shops, specialty grocery stores, cafes, and restaurants that prioritize quality, artisanal ingredients, and locally sourced products. Research establishments in your area or within your target market that have a reputation for showcasing unique and high-quality dairy products.

Once potential partners have been identified, focus on building relationships with key decision-makers such as chefs, buyers, and foodservice operators. Reach out to them directly to introduce yourself, share information about your creamery and products, and express your interest in collaborating. Attend industry events, networking mixers, or trade shows to meet potential partners in person and forge meaningful connections.

Provide samples of your dairy products to potential partners to allow them to experience the taste, quality, and versatility firsthand. Accompany your samples with product information sheets, tasting notes, and marketing materials that highlight the unique qualities and culinary applications of your products. Demonstrate how your dairy products can enhance their menu offerings, complement their existing product lineup, or differentiate their offerings from competitors.

Take the time to educate your partners about your creamery's story, production methods, and commitment to quality and sustainability. Offer insights into the sourcing of your ingredients, the craftsmanship behind your products, and any certifications or accolades your creamery has received. Help partners understand the value proposition of your dairy products and how they can resonate with their customers.

Collaborate with your partners on promotional events, menu features, or cross-promotions to generate excitement and drive sales through your partnership channels. Consider hosting tasting events, cheese pairing dinners, or cooking demonstrations featuring your dairy products at partner establishments. Work together to create special menu items, seasonal promotions, or limited-time offers that showcase your products and entice customers to try them.

Offer ongoing support to your partners by providing them with marketing materials, point-of-sale displays, and promotional assets to promote your products effectively. Stay in regular communication with your partners to gather feedback, address any concerns or questions they may have, and explore opportunities for collaboration or expansion of your partnership.

Monitor the performance of your collaborations with restaurants and specialty food retailers by tracking sales data, customer feedback, and overall engagement. Evaluate the effectiveness of different promotional initiatives, menu placements, or partnership activities to identify what works well and what can be improved. Use insights gained from your evaluations to adjust your strategies, refine your approach, and optimize future collaborations for mutual success.

By developing distribution channels, selling directly to consumers through various channels, and partnering with restaurants and specialty food retailers, you can expand your creamery's reach, increase sales opportunities, and build a loyal customer base. Embrace the diversity of distribution and sales channels available to you, experimenting with different approaches and strategies to find the optimal mix that aligns with your business goals and maximizes your creamery's potential for success.

Chapter 10: Growth and Expansion

As your creamery gains traction and establishes itself in the market, the opportunity for growth and expansion becomes increasingly viable. In this chapter, we explore strategies for scaling up production, diversifying your product line, and expanding your market reach to capitalize on emerging opportunities and propel your creamery to new heights.

Scaling Up Production

Scaling up production is a natural progression for a successful creamery aiming to meet growing demand and capitalize on economies of scale. To begin, it's crucial to evaluate your current production capacity and identify opportunities to enhance efficiency, optimize workflows, and streamline processes to accommodate higher volumes. Conduct a thorough assessment of your existing production methods, equipment utilization, and operational bottlenecks to pinpoint areas for improvement.

Investing in additional equipment, technology, and infrastructure is essential for boosting productivity and output while maintaining product quality and consistency. Consider upgrading or expanding your existing machinery, such as pasteurizers, homogenizers, and packaging equipment, to handle larger batch sizes and increased production volumes. Adopting automation and technology solutions can also help streamline production processes, minimize manual labor, and reduce the risk of errors or inconsistencies.

Moreover, it's vital to invest in infrastructure upgrades, such as additional storage facilities, refrigeration units, and transportation vehicles, to accommodate the increased volume of raw materials and finished products. Ensure that your production facility is properly equipped to handle higher throughput and storage requirements without compromising on food safety, quality, or regulatory compliance.

As you scale up production, hiring and training additional staff becomes necessary to support expanded operations effectively. Recruit skilled workers with experience in dairy processing, food safety protocols, and quality control measures to join your production team. Provide comprehensive training and ongoing support to ensure that new hires are equipped with the necessary knowledge and skills to perform their roles effectively and uphold your creamery's standards of craftsmanship and quality.

Maintaining a cohesive and well-trained workforce is essential for ensuring smooth operations, minimizing downtime, and meeting production targets consistently. Foster a culture of continuous improvement and teamwork within your production team, encouraging collaboration, open communication, and knowledge sharing to optimize workflows and address any challenges that may arise during the scaling process.

By strategically investing in equipment, technology, infrastructure, and human resources, creameries can scale up production effectively to meet growing demand while maintaining the same high standards of craftsmanship and quality that define their brand. Flexibility, adaptability, and a commitment to continuous improvement are key to successfully navigating the challenges and opportunities that come with scaling up production in the dairy industry.

Diversifying Your Product Line

Diversifying your product line is a strategic approach that enables creameries to cater to a broader range of consumer preferences, expand their customer base, and mitigate risks associated with market fluctuations or seasonal demand patterns. To begin, conducting thorough market research is essential to identify emerging trends, niche opportunities, and gaps in the market that align with your creamery's capabilities and expertise. Analyze consumer behavior, preferences, and purchasing habits to gain insights into potential areas for product expansion and innovation.

Experimenting with new flavors, formats, and product categories allows creameries to introduce innovative offerings that differentiate their brand and capture consumer interest. Consider incorporating trending ingredients, such as exotic spices, superfoods, or plant-based alternatives, into your product formulations to appeal to health-conscious consumers or those with dietary restrictions. Additionally, explore opportunities to create seasonal or limited-edition products that capitalize on seasonal trends or special occasions to drive excitement and sales.

Leveraging customer feedback and sales data is critical for refining your product development strategy and prioritizing investments in product innovation and diversification. Solicit feedback from customers through surveys, focus groups, or tasting events to understand their preferences, gather insights into their purchasing behavior, and identify areas for improvement or expansion. Analyze sales data to identify best-selling products, emerging trends, and opportunities for product line extensions or variations that align with consumer demand and market dynamics.

Furthermore, collaborating with chefs, food experts, or industry influencers can provide valuable insights and inspiration for developing new product concepts and flavor profiles. Consider partnering with local chefs or mixologists to create unique recipes or collaborations that showcase your dairy products in innovative and exciting ways. Engage with food bloggers, social media influencers, or culinary publications to generate buzz and awareness around your new product launches and attract attention from a broader audience.

By embracing a proactive approach to product innovation and diversification, creameries can stay ahead of evolving consumer preferences, differentiate their brand in the marketplace, and capitalize on emerging trends and opportunities. Continuously monitoring market dynamics, gathering customer feedback, and experimenting with new flavors and formats allow creameries to adapt and evolve their product offerings to meet the ever-changing demands of today's consumers.

Expanding Your Market Reach

Expanding your market reach is a strategic move that enables creameries to tap into new geographic markets, distribution channels, and customer segments, driving revenue growth and building brand awareness. To begin, it's essential to explore opportunities to enter new sales channels that align with your expansion goals and target demographic. Consider partnering with regional grocery chains, specialty food retailers, or international distributors to broaden your distribution network and reach customers in untapped markets.

Investing in marketing and promotional initiatives is crucial for raising awareness of your brand and products among potential customers in new markets. Utilize digital marketing strategies, such as search engine optimization (SEO), pay-per-click (PPC) advertising, and social media marketing, to extend your reach and engage with consumers online. Leverage social media platforms to share visually compelling content, behind-the-scenes stories, and user-generated content that showcase your products and highlight your brand's unique selling points.

Collaborating with influencers, food bloggers, or industry experts can also help amplify your brand's visibility and generate buzz in new markets. Partner with influencers who have a strong presence and engaged following in your target market to promote your products and introduce your brand to their audience. Host influencer events, product tastings, or virtual cooking demos to create buzz and excitement around your creamery's offerings and attract attention from potential customers.

Furthermore, developing strategic partnerships and collaborations with complementary businesses or organizations can help access new customer segments or distribution channels. Consider partnering with local cafes, restaurants, or culinary schools to feature your products on their menus or incorporate them into their recipes. Collaborate with food festivals, farmers' markets, or community events to showcase your products and connect with consumers in your target market.

By expanding your market reach through strategic partnerships, targeted marketing efforts, and innovative distribution channels, creameries can unlock new growth opportunities, attract new customers, and solidify their position in the marketplace. Continuously monitor market trends, gather feedback from customers, and adapt your strategies to meet the evolving needs and preferences of consumers in different geographic regions and market segments.

By scaling up production, diversifying your product line, and expanding your market reach, you position your creamery for sustainable growth and long-term success in the competitive dairy industry. Embrace growth and expansion as opportunities to innovate, evolve, and capitalize on emerging trends and opportunities that enable you to realize your creamery's full potential and make a lasting impact in the marketplace.

Chapter 11:
Challenges and Solutions

Running a creamery business comes with its own set of challenges, but with strategic planning and resilience, these challenges can be overcome. In this chapter, we'll address common challenges faced by creamery owners, explore strategies for overcoming obstacles, and emphasize the importance of continuous improvement and adaptation to ensure long-term success.

Addressing Common Challenges in the Creamery Business
Navigating the creamery business comes with its fair share of challenges, and being prepared to tackle them head-on is essential for success. Here are some of the common hurdles faced by creameries and effective strategies to address them:

1. Supply Chain Disruptions: One of the most common challenges in the creamery business is disruptions in the supply chain. Factors like fluctuating milk prices, delays in transportation, or shortages of key ingredients can wreak havoc on operations. To combat this, building strong relationships with reliable suppliers, diversifying your supplier base, and maintaining buffer inventory levels can help mitigate disruptions. Keeping a close eye on market trends and anticipating potential challenges will also allow for proactive management.

2. Food Safety Compliance: Maintaining compliance with food safety regulations is non-negotiable for creameries. Stringent food safety protocols and SOPs must be put in place to minimize the risk of contamination and ensure adherence to regulatory standards. Regular sanitation practices, employee training programs, and routine inspections are crucial for upholding food safety standards and protecting consumer health.

3. Seasonal Demand Variations: Creameries often face fluctuations in demand throughout the year, with peak seasons and slower periods. Adapting to these variations requires flexible production schedules, accurate demand forecasting, and diversification of product offerings. Creative marketing strategies, such as seasonal promotions or product bundling, can help stimulate sales during slower periods and maximize revenue potential.

4. Competition: Competition in the creamery business can be fierce, with numerous players vying for market share. To differentiate your brand, focus on offering unique products, maintaining exceptional quality, and investing in effective branding and marketing. Understanding consumer preferences through market research and providing outstanding customer service can help you stand out from competitors and build a loyal customer base.

5. Operational Efficiency: Maximizing operational efficiency is vital for creameries to stay competitive and profitable. Streamlining production processes, adopting automation and technology solutions, and regularly evaluating and optimizing supply chain operations are key strategies for improving efficiency. Seeking feedback from employees and implementing continuous improvement initiatives will help identify areas for enhancement and drive long-term operational success.

By recognizing these common challenges and implementing effective strategies to address them, creameries can overcome obstacles and thrive in a dynamic and competitive industry landscape. Flexibility, innovation, and a commitment to excellence are essential attributes for navigating the complexities of the creamery business successfully.

Strategies for Overcoming Obstacles

Strategies for overcoming obstacles in the creamery business require resilience, creativity, and strategic thinking to navigate challenges effectively. Here are some key approaches to address common hurdles:

1. Adaptability and Flexibility: In the face of unexpected challenges, being adaptable and flexible is crucial. Embrace change and be willing to adjust your strategies, processes, and operations as needed to overcome obstacles. Stay agile and responsive to shifting market conditions, consumer preferences, and regulatory requirements.

2. Problem-Solving and Innovation: Encourage a culture of problem-solving and innovation within your creamery. Empower employees at all levels to identify challenges, brainstorm solutions, and implement innovative ideas to overcome obstacles. Foster a collaborative environment where creativity and experimentation are valued, and reward employees for their contributions to problem-solving efforts.

3. Continuous Improvement: Commit to continuous improvement across all aspects of your creamery operations. Regularly evaluate your processes, systems, and performance metrics to identify inefficiencies, bottlenecks, and areas for enhancement. Implement feedback mechanisms to solicit input from employees, customers, and stakeholders, and use this feedback to drive meaningful improvements.

4. Risk Management: Proactively identify and mitigate potential risks that could impact your creamery's operations and profitability. Conduct risk assessments to evaluate the likelihood and potential impact of various risks, such as supply chain disruptions, regulatory changes, or market fluctuations. Develop

contingency plans and risk mitigation strategies to minimize the impact of unforeseen events and ensure business continuity.

5. Investing in Technology: Leverage technology solutions to streamline processes, improve efficiency, and enhance decision-making in your creamery. Implementing advanced software systems for inventory management, production scheduling, and quality control can help optimize operations and reduce costs. Explore opportunities to adopt emerging technologies, such as automation, data analytics, and artificial intelligence, to drive innovation and competitive advantage.

6. Building Resilience: Develop resilience as an organizational trait to withstand and bounce back from adversity. Cultivate a resilient mindset among employees by providing training, support, and resources to help them cope with challenges and setbacks. Foster a culture of resilience that encourages perseverance, adaptability, and optimism in the face of adversity.

By embracing these strategies and cultivating a proactive, resilient mindset, creameries can overcome obstacles, seize opportunities, and achieve sustainable growth and success in the dynamic and competitive dairy industry landscape. Continuously learning from experiences, adapting to change, and striving for excellence will position creameries for long-term viability and resilience in the face of challenges.

Continuous Improvement and Adaptation

In the dynamic and competitive dairy industry, the key to long-term success lies in continuous improvement and adaptation to changing market conditions. Embrace challenges as opportunities for growth and innovation, leveraging your creativity, resilience, and determination to overcome obstacles and achieve your creamery's full potential. Continuous improvement and adaptation are essential principles for success in the creamery business, allowing businesses to stay agile, responsive, and competitive in a rapidly evolving marketplace. Here are some key strategies to foster continuous improvement and adaptation:

1. Data-Driven Decision Making: Utilize data analytics and performance metrics to inform decision-making and drive continuous improvement efforts. Collect and analyze data related to production efficiency, product quality, customer feedback, and market trends to identify areas for optimization and innovation. Use this data to make informed decisions and prioritize improvement initiatives that yield the greatest impact on business performance.

2. Technology Integration: Embrace technology as a tool for improving efficiency, enhancing customer experience, and staying competitive in the market. Invest in modern dairy processing equipment, inventory management systems, and e-commerce platforms to streamline operations and optimize workflow. Leverage data analytics and business intelligence tools to track key performance metrics, identify opportunities for growth, and make data-driven decisions that drive business success.

3. Kaizen and Lean Manufacturing Principles: Implement principles of Kaizen and lean manufacturing to streamline processes, eliminate waste, and optimize efficiency in your creamery operations. Encourage employees to identify and eliminate non-value-added activities, standardize workflows, and implement visual management techniques to improve productivity and quality. Foster a culture of continuous improvement where every employee is empowered to contribute to ongoing process optimization.

4. Customer Feedback and Engagement: Actively solicit feedback from customers through surveys, reviews, and direct

communication channels to understand their needs, preferences, and expectations. Use customer feedback to identify areas for product innovation, service enhancement, and customer experience improvement. Engage with customers through social media, email newsletters, and other channels to foster meaningful relationships and gather insights that drive continuous improvement efforts.

Flexibility and Resilience: In a rapidly changing business landscape, flexibility and resilience are essential qualities for navigating challenges and seizing opportunities. Be prepared to adapt your business model, product offerings, and operational strategies in response to market dynamics, competitive pressures, and external disruptions. Cultivate a culture of resilience within your organization, fostering an environment where employees are empowered to innovate, problem-solve, and overcome obstacles with creativity and determination.

Financial Prudence: Maintain financial prudence and discipline in managing your creamery's finances, particularly during periods of uncertainty or economic downturn. Monitor key financial indicators such as cash flow, profitability, and debt levels closely, and implement cost-saving measures or adjust spending priorities as needed to maintain financial stability. Build a financial buffer or contingency fund to weather unexpected expenses or revenue fluctuations, ensuring that your creamery remains resilient and sustainable in the face of economic challenges.

5. Adaptation to Market Trends: Stay abreast of market trends, consumer preferences, and industry developments to anticipate changes and adapt your business strategies accordingly. Monitor competitor activities, industry publications, and market research reports to identify emerging trends and opportunities for innovation. Be proactive in adjusting your product offerings,

marketing strategies, and operational practices to align with evolving market dynamics and consumer demands.

6. Feedback Loops and Iterative Processes: Establish feedback loops and iterative processes within your creamery operations to facilitate continuous improvement and adaptation. Regularly review and evaluate performance metrics, customer feedback, and market trends to identify areas for refinement and adjustment. Implement mechanisms for rapid prototyping, testing, and iteration to quickly iterate on ideas and solutions and continuously enhance business processes and products.

By embracing a culture of continuous improvement and adaptation, creameries can remain resilient, innovative, and competitive in the face of evolving challenges and opportunities in the dairy industry. Prioritizing data-driven decision-making, employee empowerment, customer engagement, and market responsiveness will enable creameries to thrive in a dynamic and ever-changing business environment.

Conclusion

In the ever-evolving world of dairy production and entrepreneurship, opening and operating a successful creamery requires dedication, passion, and a strategic approach. Throughout this book, we have explored the intricacies of starting, managing, and growing a creamery business, covering everything from crafting artisanal dairy products to navigating regulatory requirements, implementing effective marketing strategies, and overcoming common challenges.

As you embark on your creamery journey, remember that success is not just about producing exceptional products—it's also about building strong relationships with customers, suppliers, and partners, fostering a culture of innovation and continuous improvement, and adapting to changing market dynamics with resilience and agility.

Whether you're a seasoned dairy professional or a novice entrepreneur, the principles and strategies outlined in this book can serve as a valuable guide to help you navigate the complexities of the creamery business and achieve your goals. Embrace the challenges, seize the opportunities, and never lose sight of your passion for creating delicious dairy products that bring joy to people's lives.

As you embark on this exciting adventure, may your creamery thrive and flourish, leaving a lasting legacy of excellence in the dairy industry. Here's to a future filled with success, innovation, and endless possibilities. Cheers to your creamery's success!